HANDS-ON HISTORY

ROMANS

DRESS, EAT, WRITE, AND PLAY JUST LIKE THE ROMANS

FIONA MACDONALD

QEB Publishing

First published in the United States by
QEB Publishing, INc.
23062 La Cadena Drive
Laguna Hills, CA 92653

www.qeb-publishing.co.uk

Library of Congress Control Number:
2007000937

ISBN 978 1 59566 619 2

Written by Fiona Macdonald
Editor Felicity Fitchard
Designer Liz Wiffen
Projects made by Veronica Erard

Publisher Steve Evans
Creative Director Zeta Davies
Senior Editor Hannah Ray

Printed and bound in China

Picture credits

Key: t = top, b = bottom, c = center, l = left, r = right,
fc = front cover

The Art Archive: p. 4 both: Musée du Louvre Paris/Dagli Orti; p. 6 tr, p. 22 bl, p. 24 tl, p. 26 tr: Archaeological Museum Naples/Dagli Orti; p. 6 br: Dagli Orti; p. 10 tr: Musée Luxembourgeois Arlon Belgium; p. 12 tl: Dagli Orti; p. 14 br: Provinciaal Museum G M Kam Nijmegen Netherlands/Dagli Orti; p. 18 bl: Archaeological Museum Cividale Friuli/Dagli Orti; p. 20 tr: Museo Civico Cristiano Brescia/Dagli Orti; p. 24 br: Musée de Cluny Paris/Dagli Orti.

Corbis: p. 12 cl: Ric Ergenbright; p. 16 tl: Robert Wallis; p. 20 br: Araldo de Luca.

Dorling Kindersley: p. 8 tl: Andy Crawford; p. 8 br, p. 12 br: Karl Shone, courtesy of the Ermine Street Guard; p. 10 bl: James McConnachie ©Rough Guides; p. 26 bl: Karl Shone; p. 28 tl: De Agostini Editore Picture Library; p. 28 bl: Gary Ombler.

Museum of London ©: p. 16 bl.

Werner Forman Archive: FC & p. 22 tr: Museo Nazionale Romano, Rome; p. 14 tl: Museo Archeologico Nazionale, Naples, Italy; p. 18 tl.

Words in **bold** are explained
in the glossary on page 30.

CONTENTS

WHO WERE THE ROMANS?

The Romans lived in central Italy, more than 2,000 years ago. Around 750 B.C.E., they founded a city called Rome. It grew fast and became rich and powerful. Roman soldiers began to fight and conquer peoples living nearby. By 100 C.E., the Romans ruled a vast empire that stretched across Europe, North Africa, and West Asia. Rome became the greatest city in the world. It had temples, theaters, shopping malls, law courts, market squares, sports **arenas**, **emperors**' palaces, and grand homes with courtyard gardens. Over a million people lived there.

A young man from Roman North Africa, painted around 2,000 years ago.

London

EUROPE

Rome

NORTH AFRICA

Rome and its empire, around 100 C.E.

Augustus became the first emperor of Rome in 27 B.C.E. He is holding a scroll (rolled-up document) to show his power as a ruler and lawmaker.

DID YOU KNOW?

IN A ROMAN LEGEND, ROME WAS BUILT BY TWINS CALLED ROMULUS AND REMUS WHO HAD BEEN BROUGHT UP BY A WOLF.

ROMAN LEGACY

Roman writers, thinkers, artists, lawmakers, builders, and engineers created a splendid civilization. It was based on their own traditions mixed with ideas borrowed from their neighbors, the Ancient Greeks. It lasted for more than 1,000 years. Many Roman ideas, inventions, and designs have survived and are still important today, such as the alphabet we use, piped water, and central heating. People in many lands still use Roman words and have Roman names such as Marcus, Antony, and Julia.

MAKE A SCROLL MAP

Make a scroll map showing the Roman Empire. For a really ancient-looking map, you can age the paper using an ordinary tea bag first.

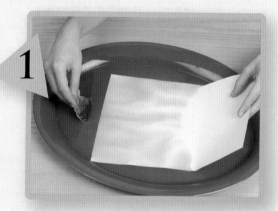

1 Put some warm water and a tea bag in a plastic tray. Add the sheet of paper.

2 After an hour, remove the paper. Blot it between two paper towels. Leave to dry.

3 From an atlas, trace a map of Europe. Color in the Roman Empire as shown on page 4.

4 Put a line of glue along one dowel. Then, carefully roll one short edge of the paper around the dowel.

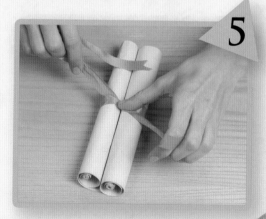

5 Repeat with the other dowel. Leave to dry. Then roll up your scroll and tie ribbon around it.

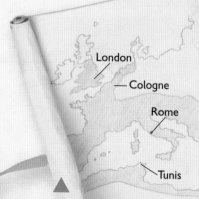

Add the names of big Roman cities, such as Rome (Italy), London (England), Cologne (Germany), and Tunis (North Africa). Use an atlas to help you.

London
— Cologne
Rome
Tunis

CITIZENS AND RULERS

Roman people were divided by birth into two groups: citizens and non-citizens. Male citizens could **vote**, own property, and get **welfare benefits**. Women and non-citizens did not have these rights. By law, women belonged to their husbands or fathers. Even so, they ran homes, set up businesses, and organized political plots. All people in the empire were made citizens in 212 C.E.

Before a Roman feast, slaves helped guests take off their outdoor clothes— and washed their feet!

DID YOU KNOW?

EMPEROR CALIGULA (37–41 C.E.) MADE HIS HORSE PRIME MINISTER. EMPEROR NERO (54–68 C.E.) SET FIRE TO ROME, THEN SANG AS HE WATCHED IT BURN.

SLAVES AND FOREIGNERS

Together with many foreigners, thousands of slaves lived in Rome and its empire. None had citizen's rights. Slaves were bought, were captured in war, or had parents who were slaves. They could be freed by their owners or purchase their freedom. Foreigners came to the empire to find work or to trade goods.

ALL-POWERFUL EMPERORS

Rome was first ruled by kings, but in 509 B.C.E., it became a **republic**. It was governed by officials chosen by the citizens and by the Senate— a group of rich, powerful men. From 27 B.C.E., Rome and its empire was ruled by emperors. Some emperors ruled well, some were mad, and some were weak or evil. After they died, all were honored as gods.

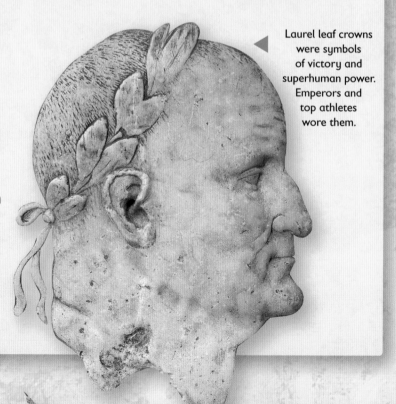

Laurel leaf crowns were symbols of victory and superhuman power. Emperors and top athletes wore them.

MAKE A
LAUREL LEAF CROWN

Make a laurel leaf crown and dress up as an all-powerful emperor. Remind everyone that the emperor's word is law!

1 Twist four pipe cleaners together in a row. Cut out a ³/₄ in. (2cm)-wide strip of the same length from green cardstock.

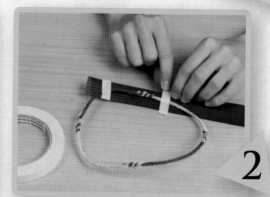

2 Twist together the ends of the pipe cleaners to make a loop. Use masking tape to attach the strip.

3 Draw a leaf onto cardboard and cut it out. This will be your template for step four.

4 Concertina fold a strip of cardstock. Draw around the template onto it. Cut the shape out, cutting through all the layers.

5 Stick each leaf to the crown with glue. Repeat step 4 to make as many leaves as you need to cover the ring.

Be like a good emperor —honest, wise, and fair. ▶

Conquering Army

To defend and expand their empire, the Romans had a well-trained, disciplined army. It was a powerful and feared fighting force. Life in the army was hard, but Roman soldiers were well paid, learned useful skills, and were rewarded with land when they retired.

Soldiers wore body armor made of tough, boiled leather or overlapping strips of metal. Their shields protected them from shoulder to knee.

DID YOU KNOW?
WHEN ATTACKING ENEMY FORTS, SOLDIERS STOOD SIDE BY SIDE AND HELD THEIR SHIELDS OVER THEIR HEADS. THIS WAS CALLED "MAKING A TORTOISE."

ARMY LIFE
The army was organized into **legions** of about 5,000 soldiers. Soldiers were put through a tough training routine. When they went on **campaign**, they carried heavy backpacks and marched as far as 19 mi. (30 km) per day. Punishments for disobeying orders were severe. If a soldier rebelled or tried to run away, one of the ten soldiers in his **troop** was killed.

A soldier's sandals were called caligae (cal-igg-eye). They had metal studs to protect the soles and stop soldiers from slipping on muddy ground.

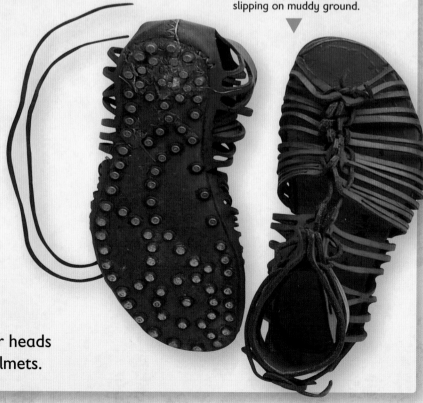

ARMY KIT
Soldiers carried a shield, sword, spear, and dagger. Underneath their armor, they wore woollen tunics, which were made from red material to hide blood. Their heads were protected by metal helmets.

MAKE A SOLDIER'S SANDALS

See how it feels to stand in a Roman soldier's shoes! Caligae were designed to bend easily so soldiers could fight, march, and run.

YOU WILL NEED:
WHITE CARDSTOCK • PENCIL
• CRAFT KNIFE • SIX 9 in. (22 cm)
LENGTHS OF RED RIBBON
• TWO 32 in. (1 m) LENGTHS
OF RED RIBBON

1

Trace each of your feet onto cardstock. Ask an adult to cut them out with a craft knife.

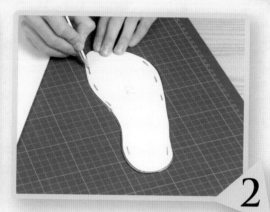

2

Label them right and left. Make four pairs of marks down each side of both card feet, as shown.

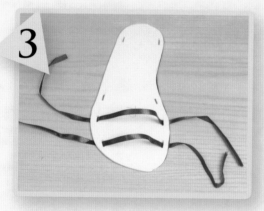

3

Ask an adult to cut slots on the marks. Feed a short ribbon through each pair of front slots on both soles.

4

Feed the long ribbon through the back slots, going under the heel. Tie the short ribbons over your feet.

5

Wrap the long ribbon around your ankle. Then feed both ends under the front short ribbon. Tie to ankle again.

To make your sandals more comfortable, you could trace your feet onto felt and glue the felt shapes to the top of the cardstock soles.

EMPIRE LANDS

The Roman Empire stretched from south Scotland and north Germany to Turkey, Egypt, and Syria. After the Romans conquered a new land, its people had to obey Roman laws, pay Roman taxes, and use Roman coins. Back in Rome, triumphal arches and columns were built to celebrate army victories. Emperors sent soldiers to live in forts all over the empire, to guard its boundaries and fight against rebels. The emperors also appointed governors to collect taxes and control conquered peoples.

This stone carving shows a Roman tax collector seated at a desk and a tax payer arguing with him!

MAKE A TRIUMPHAL ARCH

This arch still stands in the center of Rome. Make your own model of Constantine's arch in five simple steps.

YOU WILL NEED:
EMPTY CEREAL BOX • SCISSORS • PAINT AND PAINTBRUSHES • SHEET OF THIN CARDSTOCK • PENCIL • RULER • GLUE • MARKERS

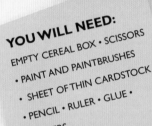

Triumphal arch made to honor Roman emperor Constantine the Great, who ruled from 324–337 C.E.

1

Cut 1/3 off an empty cereal box. Paint the rest of the box beige and leave to dry.

4

Glue the "doors" on both sides of the center arch to each other, back to back. Glue the outer "doors" to the inside of the box.

ROMAN RULE

Many different peoples lived in the empire. The Romans allowed conquered people to continue to speak their own languages, wear traditional clothes, and follow local customs. However, they also had to obey Roman laws. Roman coins were decorated with portraits of Roman rulers to remind everyone of Roman power.

GIVE AND TAKE

In some parts of the empire, such as southern Britain, Roman rulers and conquered peoples influenced one another. Some Britons learned to speak the Romans' language, Latin, and built villas and baths in the Roman style. Some Romans, meanwhile, began to wear warm British clothes, such as socks, pants, or a hooded cloak called the *birrus Britannicus*.

2

Draw three arches on cardstock and cut them out. Use this template to draw arches on the front and back of the cereal box.

3

Carefully cut ¾ of the way around each arch so you end up with six "doors."

5

Paint on the pillars and other details in white paint. Use markers to add shading above the arches.

Display your arch on a shelf or bookcase. ▶

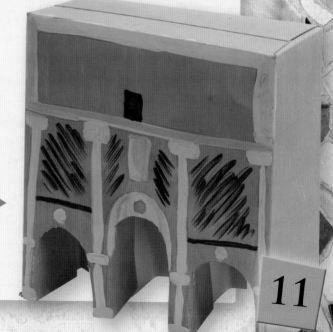

11

ROADS, FORTS, WALLS

The Romans were great builders, designers, and engineers. They made the first buildings with arches and invented domed ceilings. They experimented with new materials, such as **fired** bricks and **concrete**. As well as building roads across the empire, they built stone walls around their cities and set up army **forts** the size of small towns in newly conquered lands.

LONG, STRAIGHT ROADS

Roman builders created a road network, more than 60,000 mi. (96,000 km) long. It linked Rome with other cities in Italy and with empire lands. Each route was planned and measured by **surveyors**. They chose the shortest, straightest line between two places and constructed wood or stone bridges to carry roads across rivers. Roads were solidly built with strong **foundations** and a paved top layer.

Top picture: The Via Appia was called "the queen of roads." It ran for 363 mi. (584 km) from Rome to the coast of Italy. Bottom picture: Hadrian's Wall, in the far north of England, defended Roman empire lands from Scottish invaders.

DID YOU KNOW?

ROADS WERE A FAVORITE PLACE FOR TOMBS. PASSERS-BY WERE ASKED TO REMEMBER THE DEAD PEOPLE BURIED THERE, TO HELP KEEP THEIR SPIRITS ALIVE.

LIFE AT THE FORT

Many soldiers were trained builders as well as fighters. During peacetime, they built roads, bridges, canals, and forts. Army forts were surrounded by thick walls. Inside was everything the soldiers needed, including **barracks**, stables, baths, bakeries, hospitals, and houses for army commanders. Temples, parade grounds, and sports arenas were often built close by.

Roman soldiers marched carrying heavy backpacks loaded with a warm blanket, cooking pots, clean clothes, a spade, a pick for digging, and emergency food rations.

Send Signals Like a Roman Soldier!

Roman soldiers used flags and a code book to send each other messages when they were a long distance apart. Try it with a friend!

YOU WILL NEED:
NOTEPAPER • PEN • RULER • THIN RED CARDSTOCK • TWO 20 in. (50 cm) LENGTHS OF BAMBOO • TWO WATCHES

1

Make two matching code books with identical lists of Roman numerals and a message against each one.

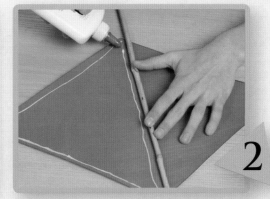

2

To make two flags, cut two large diamonds from cardstock. Fold and glue each one over a length of bamboo.

5	V
10	X
15	XV
20	XX
25	XXV
30	XXX
35	XXXV
40	XL
45	XLV

3 **Synchronize** watches and go to each end of the yard or playground. Both raise your flags and note the time.

You can make up as many messages as you like—just keep adding Roman numerals! ▶

4 Soldier One waits and looks at his or her watch while Soldier Two decides when to lower their flag.

5 When the flag goes down, Soldier One checks how many seconds have passed (e.g. 5), finds the numeral in his code book (5 = V) and reads the message ("Want to play a game?").

V	WANT TO PLAY A GAME?
X	SEND MORE SUPPLIES
XV	EMPEROR CLOSE
XX	CHECK THAT YOUR SANDALS ARE TIED
XXV	ENEMIES ON HORIZON
XXX	TIME FOR A SNACK

Write these messages in your code book or make up your own funny ones.

CLEVER CALCULATION

THE ROMANS ALSO AMAZED THEIR FRIENDS WITH THIS TRICK!

THINK OF A NUMBER
MULTIPLY IT BY 3
DIVIDE IT BY 2
MULTIPLY IT BY 3
DIVIDE IT BY 9
MULTIPLY IT BY 2
THIS SHOULD GIVE YOU THE NUMBER YOU FIRST THOUGHT OF!

LATIN AND LEARNING

Roman portrait of a woman writing poetry. She is using a pointed stick, called a stylus, to write on a wax-covered tablet.

The Romans spoke Latin. Most ordinary Roman people could not read or write. Only children from rich families went to school. Both boys and girls went to primary school, called a ludus (loo-duss). Pupils were taught reading, writing, and arithmetic. At 11, boys went on to secondary school, called a grammaticus (gram-at-ee-cus). They studied history, law, and public speaking.

LATIN

Latin was the official language of government, trade, and learning throughout the empire. Trained writers, called **scribes**, used Latin to keep lists of taxes, new laws, army battles, emperor's **reigns**, and other important events. Sometimes, owners taught their slaves to read and write. Many scribes were slaves. Roman writers wrote poems, plays, celebrity life stories, exciting histories, cookbooks, and **inscriptions** in Latin.

DID YOU KNOW?

MANY LANGUAGES STILL CONTAIN LATIN WORDS. CASTLE, MEMORY, MONSTER, MILE, PLUMBER, TRIUMPH, ULTIMATE, AND EXTRAORDINARY ALL COME FROM LATIN.

Pupils and scribes jotted down notes on wax-covered tablets like this one.

LASTING LANGUAGE

Traders learned Latin to speak to Roman rulers and to people from distant parts of the empire. Latin slowly spread to many parts of Europe. Some languages today, such as French, Spanish, and Italian, are based on Latin. English contains many Latin words, too.

MAKE A ROMAN PLAQUE

Practice your Latin by making a Roman plaque for your bedroom door. Inscribe it with "Salvete amici," which means "Greetings, friends!"

YOU WILL NEED:
AIR-DRYING CLAY • ROLLING PIN • RULER • PLASTIC KNIFE • MODELING TOOL • PENCIL • PAINT AND PAINTBRUSHES • LENGTH OF STRING

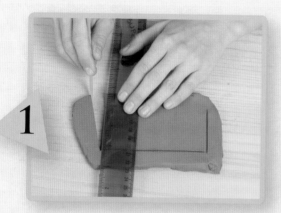

1 Roll out a ½ in. (1cm)-thick slab of clay. Use a plastic knife to cut out a 6 x 3 in. (16 x 8 cm) rectangle.

2 With a modeling tool, draw a ¾ in. (2 cm) border. In the center of the plaque, inscribe your Latin message.

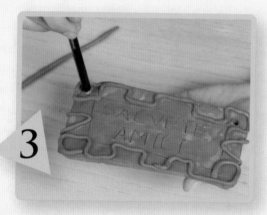

3 Add pieces of clay to build up the border. With a sharp pencil, make a hole in each of the top corners.

4 When your tablet is completely dry, paint it using Roman colors, such as black, red, and white.

5 Once the paint is dry, thread the string through both holes, tie the ends together, and hang up.

SALVETE AMICI

Copy the Roman-style letters shown here to make your plaque as realistic as possible.

15

KEEPING CLEAN

The Roman baths at Aquae Sulis (Ak-way Soo-liss), now known as the city of Bath, in England. The pools are filled by natural hot springs.

The Romans used their engineering skills to keep their cities clean. They built **aqueducts** to bring fresh drinking water into their towns and cities. Water flowed from fountains in the street for everyone to use. The Romans built public toilets with rows of seats side by side, and dug huge underground sewers to carry human waste away. Most important of all, they built splendid public baths in cities and towns.

PLAY TROPA!

While they were relaxing at the baths, men loved to play dice and board games. Tropa! was one of their favorites.

YOU WILL NEED:
AIR-DRYING CLAY · MODELING TOOLS · SMALL PIECE OF DOWEL · OLD WATER BOTTLE TOP · 4 DICE PER PLAYER · ACRYLIC PAINT

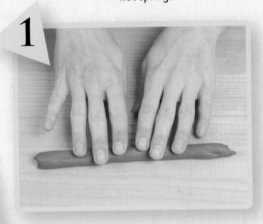

1

Warm up the clay in your hands. Then, roll out several long, thin clay "sausages."

This dice pot was found in Roman London, which was called Londinium.

3

Push the dowel into the pot and press the clay in around the join. Then, smooth out the pot's sides.

AT THE BATHS

The Romans thought that being clean kept them healthy, so they went to the baths several times a week. Women bathed in the morning; men in the afternoon. First, bathers took off their clothes and smeared themselves with olive oil. They played sports or did exercises, then got a slave to scrape the oil, dirt, and sweat from their skin with a **strigil**. After this, they entered the bathing rooms.

HOT AND COLD

Bathers went to the tepidarium (warm room), then to the caldarium (hot room, with a pool). They might enjoy a steam bath in the sudatorium (sweat room), chat with friends, or have a massage before cooling off in the tepidarium. Then, they'd plunge into the frigidarium (cold pool). Relaxed and refreshed, they put on their clothes and might visit the baths' hairdresser, snack bar, or library.

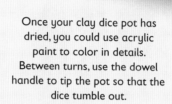

DID YOU KNOW?
THE ROMANS DIDN'T HAVE TOILET PAPER —THEY USED A SPONGE ON A STICK INSTEAD!

Once your clay dice pot has dried, you could use acrylic paint to color in details. Between turns, use the dowel handle to tip the pot so that the dice tumble out.

2

Fold in one end of a "sausage" and coil the rest. Add more "sausages" to build up the pot's shape.

4

Use a modeling tool to draw two parallel lines around the rim. Trace a bottle top to make circles.

HOW TO PLAY

RULES FOR TWO PLAYERS

Each player takes turns throwing their four dice, one by one, into the upright cup. It isn't as easy as it sounds! At the end of each round, each player adds up the numbers on any dice that have landed inside the cup. If your score is higher than your partner's, take one of their dice. The winner ends up with all the dice.

Some combinations had names:
Venus – any four without a 6 e.g. 5, 4, 2, 1
Senio – four including a 6 e.g. 6, 4, 2, 1
Vulture – four the same e.g. 6, 6, 6, 6
Dog – lowest possible score e.g. 1,1,1,1
If you throw a venus, a senio, a vulture, or a dog, double your score!

17

Town and Country Life

I n the city of Rome, poor families lived together in blocks of apartments about six stories high, called insulae (which means "islands"). There were shops and inns on the noisy, busy ground floors. The top floors were damp and drafty in winter but unbearably hot in the summer. Other families lived in rooms behind their shops or workshops, or built little wooden huts in back streets.

Emperor Hadrian's villa was famous for its beautiful gardens filled with marble statues of gods and goddesses.

CITY DANGERS
Many city districts were overcrowded, smelly, and dirty. Disease spread quickly—in 165 C.E., thousands of Romans were killed by plague. At night, criminals, beggars, and spies lurked in dark alleyways.

Villas often had decorative mosaic floors. The patterns or pictures were made from hundreds of tiny tiles called tesserae (tess-urr-aye).

TRANQUIL VILLAS
Rich Romans lived in fine town houses, with large rooms and private courtyard gardens. They also built large country homes, called villas, in many parts of the empire. Villas were surrounded by gardens, ponds, orchards, stables, and farms. Some villa owners grew grain for sale, made wine, or raised cattle. Others used their villas to impress powerful people visiting from Rome.

18

MAKE A ROMAN MOSAIC

Make a beautiful mosaic of a god. You might want to practice arranging your tesserae before you glue them down.

YOU WILL NEED:
TURQUOISE, RED, YELLOW, AND BROWN PAPER • SCISSORS • COMPASS • 8 x 8 in. (20 x 20 cm) WHITE CARDSTOCK • PENCIL • PROTRACTOR • COLORED PAPER SCRAPS • GLUE

1

Cut tiny squares from colored paper. Set compass to 2 in. (5 cm). Draw a circle in the middle of the white cardstock.

2

Mark off 30° intervals around the circle. Draw a line from each mark to the edge of the square.

3

Glue turquoise squares in every other section around the circle. Leave slight gaps between squares.

4

Glue yellow squares in the circle. Stick red squares in the empty sections and brown squares around the circle.

5

Draw the nose, eyes, lips, eyebrows, and swirls on colored paper. Cut them out and glue them in place.

Use adhesive putty to hang your mosaic on the wall for everyone to admire!

19

FAMILY LIFE

Family life was important to the Romans. Family members often worked together, in politics, in business, or on farms. They believed it was their duty to protect one another, and help each other in any way that they could. Families also said prayers together, to honor dead **ancestors**.

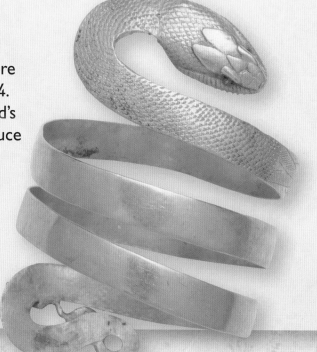

A Roman mother and her children. They came from a rich family. You can see that the girl is wearing beautiful jewels.

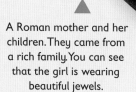

FAMILY ROLES

Roman families could be large, with parents, grandparents, children, cousins, aunts, uncles, and slaves all living in the same building. Each family was led by a man called the "paterfamilias"—the father of a family. In law, he had total power over family members but it was Roman women who had most day-to-day control. They did the cooking, cleaning, childcare, and many other essential tasks—or organized slaves to do them.

MARRIAGE

Roman marriages were arranged by parents, for political or money-making reasons. Girls could marry when they were 12 years old and boys when they were 14. The new bride went to live in her husband's family home. Her main duty was to produce sons, to keep the family name alive. Later she might come to love her husband, though this did not always happen.

A Roman woman's gold bracelet, shaped like a snake. For the Romans, snakes were symbols of good luck. They were also painted on walls and added to mosaic floor patterns.

20

MAKE A
SERPENT ARM BRACELET

Swirling snake bracelets were popular with Roman women. Snakes were a symbol of good health for the woman and her family.

YOU WILL NEED:
2 PIPE CLEANERS • RULER • PENCIL • GOLD CARDSTOCK • SCISSORS • MASKING TAPE • GLUE • FINE TIP BLACK MARKER

1

Twist two pipe cleaners together. Measure the length of the two pipe cleaners.

2

Draw two rectangles on gold cardstock that are each the same length as the pipe cleaners and $\frac{1}{2}$ in. (1.5 cm) wide.

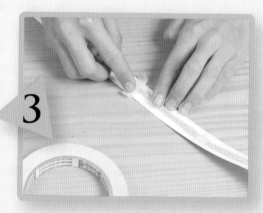

3

Use masking tape to attach the pipe cleaners to the back of one rectangle. Glue the other on top.

4

Using the black marker, draw a snake's head. Then add the body and swirly tail.

Wear your serpent on your upper arm like a Roman!

▼

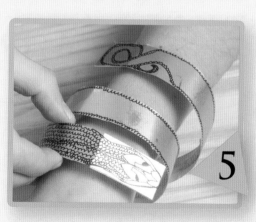

5

Curl the snake around your lower arm. When it's the right shape, you can push it to the top of your arm.

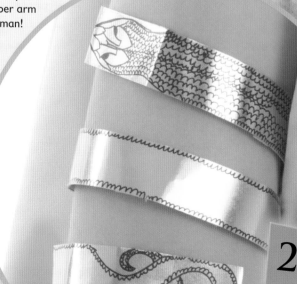

21

GODS AND SPIRITS

The Romans were religious people. They believed that many different gods and spirits watched over them and controlled their lives. Venus was goddess of love, Neptune was god of the sea, Mars (the Romans' favorite) was god of war. Mighty Jupiter, lord of the sky, was king of all the gods. Roma was the spirit of the city of Rome. Good things, such as peace, were also **worshiped**.

▲ Many Roman soldiers worshiped Mithras, shown above, a god from Persia (Iran). His followers believed he would give them life after death.

YOU WILL NEED:
PENCIL • GOLD CARDSTOCK • RULER • COMPASS • SCISSORS • DOUBLE-SIDED TAPE • 14 in. (35 cm) LENGTH OF STRING • VELCRO® SPOT • DECORATIVE BUTTON

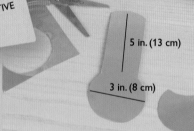

1

5 in. (13 cm)

3 in. (8 cm)

MAKE A LUCKY BULLA

All children carried a lucky charm around their neck, kept safely inside a pouch called a bulla. Rich children's bullas were often made of gold.

Copy the big shape and the circle shape onto gold cardstock. Cut them out.

4

Repeat step 3 to add the front of the bulla. Then loop the string and tape in place, as shown.

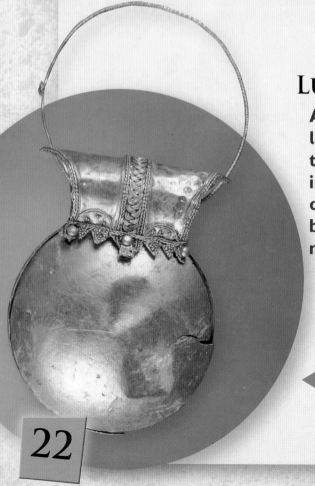

◄ This gold bulla has a loop so that it could be hung around a child's neck. It would have contained a charm shaped like a snake or another symbol of long life.

TEMPLES AND PRAYERS

The Romans built splendid temples at the heart of their cities as homes for their gods. Priests and priestesses said prayers and offered **sacrifices** there. They also examined the insides of sacrificed animals to foretell the future. On festival days, they led processions through the streets with music and dancing.

OFFERINGS, CHARMS, AND GHOSTS

The Romans believed in Lares and Penates, household gods who protected their homes. They built shrines to them in their houses and left offerings there every day. They wore lucky charms, or jewelry shaped like magic animals, to scare away ghosts and demons that brought bad luck. Roman people also loved poems and stories about gods, magic, and monsters.

Cut out a 10 x 1 in. (25 x 3 cm) strip of cardstock. Draw about a $1/4$ in. ($1/2$ cm) margin on each side. Cut zig-zags up to each margin.

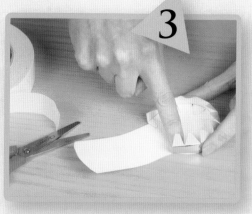

Fold in all the zigzag tabs. Stick the tabs to the back of the big shape, as shown. Stick down a few at a time.

Curve the top of the bulla over and add a Velcro® spot to attach it to the front. Glue on a decorative button.

From felt or cardstock, cut out a tiny charm, shaped like a flower, a snake, or a star, to go inside your bulla.

▼

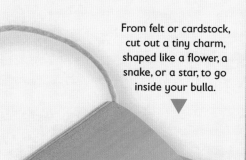

> ## CURSES!
> ROMANS ASKED THEIR FAVORITE GODS AND GODDESSES TO HELP THEM—AND HARM THEIR ENEMIES! THEY WROTE CURSES ON THIN SHEETS OF LEAD (SOFT METAL) AND LEFT THEM AT HOLY PLACES, ESPECIALLY WOODS AND SPRINGS.

Clothes, Hair, Jewelry

Roman men and women liked to follow fashion. Clothes styles stayed the same for hundreds of years but there were often new designs in jewelry, hair, and beards. Women and slaves wove wool, linen, and silk to make clothing. From leather, craftsmen made sandals for indoor wear and flat boots for outdoor wear.

Roman women wore their long hair arranged in many complicated styles. Roman men were clean shaven with short hair, except around 100–200 C.E., when they preferred longer curls and beards.

DID YOU KNOW?

ROMAN WOMEN WORE WIGS! THE WIGS WERE MADE FROM DARK HAIR PURCHASED FROM INDIA OR FROM BLONDE HAIR CUT FROM GERMAN CAPTIVES AND SLAVES.

MEN'S CLOTHES

Men wore sleeveless, knee-length tunics. In cold weather, men wore a short cloak over their tunic. On special occasions, citizens wore woollen **togas**, but they were difficult to put on and awkward to move around in. Togas were usually white, but senators' and emperors' togas were edged with expensive purple dye.

WOMEN'S FASHION

Women's clothes covered them from head to toe. They wore an undertunic, a long, loose dress called a stola, and a palla (shawl) draped over their hair and shoulders. Girls' clothes were white, but married women could wear bright colors. Grown women also wore white face powder, black eyeliner, red lip paint, and pink rouge.

This dog-shaped brooch was used to fasten a Roman robe. It is made of bronze and decorated with enamel (colored glass).

MAKE A
ROBE CLASP

Romans did not have zippers or buttons. They used clasps and brooches instead. Make a stunning dog clasp for your Roman robe!

YOU WILL NEED:
PENCIL • TRACING PAPER • WHITE PENCIL • BLACK CARDSTOCK • SCRAPS OF GOLD FOIL • SCISSORS • GLUE • COLORED PAPER • GOLD PEN • SAFETY PIN • TAPE • BLACK FINE TIP MARKER

1 Draw or trace the dog shape onto black cardstock and go over it in white pencil. Cut it out with scissors.

2 Draw the body shape and eye on gold foil and cut out. Now glue them onto your black dog shape.

3 Cut out small shapes from colored paper. Arrange and then glue them onto the gold panel.

4 Use a gold pen to add teeth, a collar, and details to the ears and legs. Draw a solid black circle on the eye.

5 Use a small piece of masking tape to attach a safety pin to the back of your cloak clasp.

Romans used clasps to hold their cloaks together, but you could pin yours to a white sheet worn as a toga. ▶

EATING AND DRINKING

Most Romans ate just one main meal, in mid-afternoon, when the day's work was over. They might also have a light snack at breakfast and dinner times. Romans did not like to eat too much. It was considered unhealthy, greedy, and impolite.

A Roman man buys bread for his son. You can see the baker behind his shop counter and stacks of freshly baked round loaves. ▶

FAST FOOD

Most Romans were too poor to have a kitchen in their home, but some families heated food over pots of glowing charcoal. This caused many fires. Instead of cooking, Romans bought baked bread, fruit, and cheese from market stalls. They also bought hot soups and bean stews from their nearest fast food shop, or popina (pop-ee-nah).

DID YOU KNOW?
THE ROMANS ATE DORMICE, SOWS' UDDERS, SEA URCHINS, AND GARUM—A SAUCE MADE FROM ROTTEN FISH.

◀ Rich Romans ate rare, luxury foods, such as song-birds and asparagus. Food was often served on red clay dishes, made in France.

FASHIONABLE FEASTS

Wealthy Roman families had kitchens, storerooms, and slaves to cook and serve fine food and wine. Rich Romans liked to experiment with different flavors, such as sweet and sour or salty and spicy. Fashionable Romans loved dinner parties. These were held in special dining rooms, where guests reclined (leaned over) on couches to eat and discuss the latest news or ideas.

MAKE SWEET HONEY TOAST

The Romans ate fruit, nuts, and small sweet treats after a meal. Make delicious honey toast for your bellarium (dessert)!

YOU WILL NEED:
CUTTING BOARD • 4 SLICES OF BREAD • KNIFE • BOWL • 1 ¼ CUPS (300 ML) MILK • OLIVE OIL • FRYING PAN • HONEY • TEASPOON • SIDE PLATES • NAPKINS

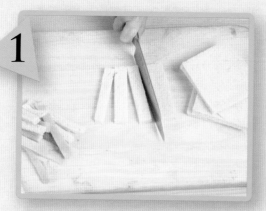

1

Ask an adult to remove the crusts from the bread and cut the bread into ½ in. (1.5 cm)-wide strips.

2

Pour milk into a bowl. Dip each strip of bread into the milk, then put the strips on a plate.

3

Ask an adult to lightly fry the strips in olive oil until they start to toast and turn golden.

Everyone will want to try some sweet honey toast—make sure you've got enough to go around!

▼

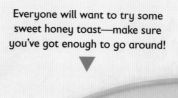

4

Ask an adult to put them on a plate. Then drip honey over them and serve. You'll need napkins for sticky fingers!

AT THE GAMES

All Romans loved sports and games. Men rode horses, played hockey, rowed boats, and wrestled. Young women ran races and lifted weights. Everyone gambled on dice. Most of all, the Romans loved watching contests between sportsmen, such as gladiators. These were strong men or prisoners who fought to the death in front of huge, cheering crowds.

There were five different kinds of gladiators. This Retarius (Net-man) has no helmet or body armor. His only weapons are a spear and a net.

YOU WILL NEED:

BIG SHEET OF CARDBOARD • RULER • SCISSORS • MARKER • PAINT AND PAINTBRUSHES • COMPASS • DOUBLE-SIDED TAPE • WHITE CARDSTOCK

1

Cut a 24 x 16 in. (60 x 40 cm) rectangle from cardboard. Inside the rectangle, draw a big oval that touches the edges.

DRESS AS A GLADIATOR

A gladiator's shield was his best friend—it was the only thing between him and certain death!

This Secutor (Pursuer) gladiator wears a heavy helmet and metal leg guards. He is armed with a sharp sword and protected by a huge, curved shield.

4

Draw 4 in. (10 cm)-diameter circle on cardstock. Cut it out, paint it brown, and when it's dry, stick it to the center of the shield.

GLADIATORS

Fights between gladiators, or between gladiators and wild animals, were held in open-air arenas. The largest, the Colosseum in Rome, could hold around 60,000 spectators. Women were allowed in, as well as men, but had to sit at the back. Top gladiators became very famous, but their fights were savage, bloodthirsty, and cruel. So many animals were shipped from Africa to be slaughtered, that some species became **extinct**.

CHARIOT RACING

On public holidays, crowds hurried to their local sports stadium to watch daring chariot races. Chariots pulled by horses dashed around oval racecourses called hippodromes. In Rome, charioteers drove for rival teams, such as the Reds, Whites, Greens, and Blues. The best charioteers were superstars, but racing was dangerous. Men and horses were often killed in crashes.

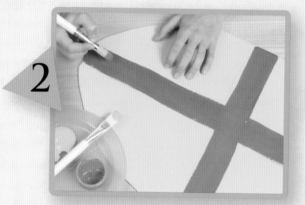

2

Cut out the oval, then paint it yellow and let it dry. Now, paint on a red cross as shown.

3

Paint two diagonal lines that cross in the middle. Now paint a red border around the rim.

5

Cut out a rectangle of cardstock. Use it to make an arm handle on the back, as shown.

Feel as brave as a gladiator as you carry your shield. ▶

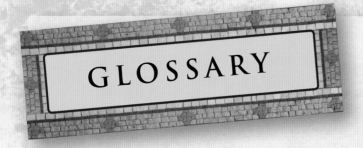
GLOSSARY

ancestors Family members who lived and died many years ago.

aqueduct A high bridge designed to carry water over land.

arena A big building with many rows of seats around a large, open area. Designed for playing and watching sports and gladiator contests.

barracks A large building for soldiers to live in.

campaign Organized army action, such as a long march or an invasion.

concrete A Roman building material made by mixing crushed stone with water and leaving the mixture to set. Today, concrete is made from sand, gravel, cement, and water.

emperor All-powerful ruler of the Roman Empire.

extinct A plant or animal that no longer exists.

fired When clay is baked in a very big, hot oven.

forts Big army camps where Roman soldiers lived in conquered lands.

foundations Bottom layer of a building, which supports everything above it.

inscriptions Writing carved on stone.

legions Units in the Roman army, containing around 5,000 soldiers.

reign Length of time that a ruler stays in power.

republic System of government without a king or emperor. It gives power to ordinary people.

sacrifice Killing people or animals to please the gods.

scribe Trained man or woman who reads and writes to earn a living.

strigil A body scraper with a curved blade, also used by the Ancient Greeks.

surveyor Person skilled at measuring buildings and land.

synchronize Set to the same time.

toga Large piece of fabric worn by Roman senators and emperors, also worn by citizens on special occasions.

troop A group of soldiers.

vote Choose a leader or a representative.

welfare benefits Food or money given by governments to people in need to help them survive.

worship To respect or love a god.

INDEX

NOTES FOR PARENTS AND TEACHERS

• Many Latin names, words, and phrases are still used today. Visit a library and find a book of children's names and a good dictionary. Use them to help children make a list of Latin names and words that they already use or would like to learn. You can find similar information from the following Web sites for adults: http://www.krysstal.com/borrow_latin.html, http://www.krysstal.com/wordname_latin.html and http://www.phrases.org.uk/meanings/latin-phrases.html.

• All around the world, enthusiasts have set up groups to relive the Roman past. Many give public displays; some also visit schools. Parents and teachers can find information about reenactment groups in many different countries at http://www.romanempire.net/romepage/Links/roman_reenactment_groups.htm. Many groups also have their own Web sites: http://www.vicus.org.uk (civilian life) and http://www.esg.ndirect.co.uk (the Roman Army).

• The Romans loved taking part in sports. Research some Roman ball games, such as harpastum or trigon, at the library or online. Encourage the children to set up teams with Roman place or personal names and have a go. If you can't find the exact rules, you may need to improvise.

Useful Web sites

Many children are fascinated by Roman gladiators and soldiers. With your help, these Web sites should answer most of their questions:
• http://ablemedia.com/ctcweb/consortium/gladiators.html
• http://penelope.uchicago.edu/~grout/encyclopaedia_romana/gladiators/gladiators.html
• http://museums.ncl.ac.uk/archive/arma/welc/beginner/faq1.htm

These Web sites about all aspects of Roman life are designed for the children to use by themselves:
• http://www.historyforkids.org/learn/romans/index.htm
• http://www.bbc.co.uk/schools/romans/

This site has a simple Roman number game for the children to play:
• http://www.learnenglish.org.uk/words/activities/romandr.html

This Web site lets children play samples of real Roman music and find out about Roman musical instruments:
• http://www.ancestral.co.uk/romanmusic.htm